THE

SUCCESSFUL

REAL ESTATE AGENT

COPYRIGHT MAY 2010

BY

GARY CASEY

1-428538091

ISBN 1453630406

INTRODUCTION

This publication was written to help people who are interested in getting into the Real Estate Business or are in the Real Estate business now. So many people fail at trying to be a Real Estate agent and even end up going into big debt. The reason for this is they do not understand that being a Real Estate agent is not just a sales position but also a business.

People just getting into the business need to be educated on what it takes to start and run a small business. This is one of the biggest reasons people fail. I hope that what I have written in this publication will help. It is hard to get the right information. The Real Estate books on the market are out of date. The things they are telling people to do to be successful are things that were done years ago. A lot of things have changed. The day of cold calling and knocking doors are over. There are new rules and laws. The computer and the internet have changed a lot of things. It has changed the way we advertise and the way we communicate. The rise and fall of the Real Estate market the last few years has also changed a lot of things. Homes are not selling the way they once were and that has affected how many Real Estate agents there are in the work force.

Changing conditions can make it even harder to make it in the Real Estate business. That's why you need to be doing the right things.

I first became a Licensed Real Estate Agent in 1987 in Kansas City Missouri. Shortly after that I went to Central Florida and have been selling Real Estate here ever since. I have over 20 years experience.

I have seen every kind of market both good and bad. I can remember in Kansas City in 1987 interest rates were 16% and it was diffidently a buyer's market. Even when you sold a house it was very hard to get it financed. Then around 2004 the market was just the opposite, more so in Florida. Houses were selling fast and prices were going up rapidly. It was a seller's market and the competition for listings was huge.

In the over 20 years that I have been in the business I have seen every kind of Real Estate Agent you can imagine. I have learned from every one of them, all of the good things as well as the bad things. I know what works and what doesn't. I have also read a lot of Real Estate Books over the years. Most of them say all the same things. Most of which don't work in the real world. They ramble on and on about nothing.

I have put together this publication to tell people who are interested in making a career as a Real Estate Agent the real simple truth about what it takes. It can be a wonderful career if you put enough into it and give it time to build.

I wish someone had shared this kind of information with me when I started. Then it wouldn't have taken me all these years to figure it out.

TABLE OF CONTENTS

CHAPTER
1

GETTING STARTED IN THE REAL ESTATE BUSINESS

1.REAL ESTATE IS A BUSINESS

2.PICKING A REAL ESTATE COMPANY

3.WHAT IS A REAL ESTATE BROKER

REAL ESTATE IS A BUSINESS

Lots of people think that being a Real Estate Agent is strictly a sales position. You simply get a Real Estate License and go to work for a Real Estate Broker or National Real Estate Company and that's it. Nothing could be farther from the truth.

There are lots of sales jobs where you go to work for a company selling all sorts of products. The company pays you a salary, helps you get leads, and gives you a supervisor to train you how to get sales.

When you are a Real Estate Agent you have none of these. The product you sell is yourself. The Broker tells you that he or she will help you get sales, but you will find that this is most always a false statement. In fact you will find that a lot of Brokers sell Real Estate themselves and are actually part of your competition. They will train you how to fill out paperwork, work the fax machine, and that's about it.

Being a Real Estate Agent is a business and the faster you learn and accept that the better off you are. You are on your own and figuring out how to pay your bills and have the money to start your business should be your main concern. It takes a while to build any business. You may have to start part time and only go full time when your business will support you. It depends on how much money you have or can get to start your business.

Real Estate is a 7 day a week job 24/7. Even if you have to work a part time job to get started you are still a full time Real Estate Agent. I am not saying you will have to work part time, but I have known a lot of agents who have started that way and have been very successful.

You must think like a business. Think of it like starting a Fast Food Restaurant. First you have to have money for equipment and supplies. You have to have a great product and you also need to have great advertising. You can have the best hamburger in the country, but it's not going to do you any good if nobody knows about it.

The same is true when you are a Real Estate Agent. The product is you and what you offer your customers. At the same time your product can't be what everybody else is offering. There is a lot of competition for the business in Real Estate.

If I ask you for $20 and said I would give you $100 in return would you do it? Of course you would. That is a sample of how the Real Estate Business works. Like any other business there is a cost of your product. Just like you buying a hamburger patty for $.40, cooking it, and selling it for $1.00.

There is a cost of goods in Real Estate. You have to have money to get started. There is a cost of your license, business cards, and other office supplies. The most important and biggest cost is the cost of advertising. Just like starting any other business you have to have a way to get new costumers. People who start new businesses apply for a business loan, have some money already, or start part time.

You can expect to put in $20.00 for every $100.00 you make. In this publication I will tell you where to put that money and also not to waste time doing things that won't make you money unless you have that time to waste.

PICKING A REAL ESTATE COMPANY

Getting started toward being a Real Estate Agent can be confusing. It is hard to figure out what to do first. The questions are, How do I get my License?, How do I pick a Real Estate Company?, and How much money will I have to have?

The first thing you do is pick a Real Estate Company. This is a simple process. Look for the Companies in your area that are convenient for you to work for. Consider how far the office is from you since you will be going there a lot. Consider how active they are in the area. Consider how much advertising they do.

It is best to pick a National Company if possible. This will help you to get listings, because people list their homes with companies they recognize. These companies usually have more advertising money to spend also.

It is wise to interview with more than one since different companies offer different things. Real Estate Companies offer different commission plans to start. They offer different kinds of floor duty. You need to find out if they have an open floor or a closed floor. An open floor means that they let the agents on duty take sales calls on listed properties even if they are not yours. A closed floor means that all sales calls will be forwarded to the listing agent. You need to find out how much advertising they do for you. You also need to find out if they allow you to set your own commission because you might want to take some listings at a lower commission to get started.

Let's start with commission plans. Most companies start out a new agent with about 50% of the commission that comes into the company from any sale that is generated by a new agent. I have seen some companies start new agents up to as much as 70% of the commission. That's why you have to interview more than one.

There are two sides of what is best considering an open floor verses a closed floor. A lot of new agents like an open floor because it can lead them to new clients. The company makes out a floor schedule and each agent gets an equal amount of shifts. I personally do not like an open floor because you have to put in a lot of time doing nothing. To me it is non productive and the amount of calls I got when I did floor didn't generate many sales. I am more of a listing agent so I like all sales calls that come in on my listings to come to me, which is a closed floor.

Find out how much company paid advertising they offer. This is very important. You have enough expense as it is. They certainly can pay for your listing being advertised in magazines and newspapers. This is an important issue to sellers when they list their home with you. They want to know where it is going to be advertised.

A very important thing to remember is that Real Estate is a business. You are the one paying most of the expenses as you go such as advertising etc. and you don't get paid until you sell something. The

Real Estate Broker or Company isn't paying you a salary, but they receive a large portion of your commission. They should let you be in control of your business. If they want to control you and tell you what to do, go on to the next Company or Broker down the street. Companies and Brokers need agents! You are valuable.

I will give you a good example. When you start you need business. The best way to get business is having listings and you will hear me talk about this over and over again. To start out you might want to take a listing for less commission. Suppose that the going commission rate in your area is 7%. You might want to take some listings at 4 ½%. This will help you compete and get the listing over your competition. If the broker will not allow you to do this, you need go down the street and find another Company or Broker.

Another example is you might want to offer the seller the ability to cancel your listing agreement at any time if he or she is not satisfied with your service. This is a very helpful tool to getting listings. These are just a couple of tools you need to get business. If the Company you choose will not allow you to do these things than you do not want to sign up with them. Again this is your own business. Whether you succeed or fail depends on you. A Real Estate Broker or Company is just interested on how many agents they can get. The more they get the more money they make and they really are not concerned whether you make it or not.

Sometimes it is almost better to go with a smaller company if they will give you some freedom to run your own business.

After you decide what Company to go with it is time to get your Real Estate License. Interviewing companies first was important because it will let you know if you want to proceed with being a Real Estate Agent.

It is best to attend a Real Estate School in your area that will train you on how to pass your Real Estate Exam.

WHAT IS A REAL ESTATE BROKER

When you go to work for a Real Estate Company you will find a Real Estate Broker in that company. This person is usually the manager but not always. A person that has a brokers license can have Real Estate Agents work for them. They are responsible for the Real Estate Agents under them. It can vary from state to state on how long you have to be a Real Estate Agent before you can get your brokers license. In my state it is 2 years. After 2 years you can get your brokers license and start your own

Real Estate Company.

When you are starting out it is best to pick a national real estate company. They usually have some training classes and it is easier to get people to list their houses with a company they recognize. They have some good training classes and the broker is usually the owner because a lot the offices are individually owned.

You need to understand what you need the broker for because you are going to be paying them a lot of money with your commission splits. They should be training you on how to fill out real estate contracts and how to handle different phases of the real estate transaction. They should also pay for advertising your listings.

Even though they are supposed to be training you on how to get business, most brokers teach the same old things that they have taught for years. They tell you to get on the phone and call expired listings and for sale by owners. They tell you to hold open houses and do floor time at the office. They teach you everything except how to run a successful Real Estate business. New agents usually do these things for a couple of months until they realize that are putting in a lot of time and not making any money.

The only thing I need a broker for is to carry my Real Estate License and pay for advertising on my listings. Everything else is up to me. In fact the only time I go to the office is to meet with a client. I do everything else at my home office.

I have known some successful agents who got their brokers license, and started their own real estate company. In my state you have to have a place of business to have your own company. This is a business location with a sign out front stating the name of your business. You can do this by going to a title company, a lawyer's office, or other business that have an office with a conference room and offer to pay them rent for the use of the conference room. They would also need to let you put a small sign by the front door with the name of your business on it and let you receive mail at the location. You can do everything at you office in your home. The only reason you would go to your business location is to meet with a client or to pick up your mail. I hardly ever meet a client at the office. Most times I meet them at their homes.

I know a very successful person in my area that has her own company. She uses a lot of the ideas I state in this publication. While it is harder for her to get listings than a national company she offers the sellers a lot more than they do and at a lower price. Since she is the broker she can advertise anything she wants without any other brokers permission.

This could certainly be your goal and a way to own your own business.

CHAPTER
2

GETTING THE BUSINESS

1.WAYS TO GET NEW BUSINESS

2.DIRECT MAIL, OPEN HOUSES

FRIENDS AND RELATIVES,

3.FLOOR TIME AND WEBSITES,

4.NEWPAPERS AND

EXPIRED LISTINGS

5. COLD CALLING

WAYS TO GET NEW BUSINESS

Now we get down to some of the real truths about what it takes to be a successful Real Estate Agent. The two main things to know is how much business you need and how are you going to get that business.

It takes 12 sales a year to gross $30,000. That is an average sale of a $150,000 house and an average net commission of $2500.00. per house Therefore it would take 24 sales to gross $60,000 In your area it might be more or less. Your expenses are 20% of your gross. That means you will have to spend $6000.00 to gross $30,000.00 and $12000.00 to gross $60,000.00. This is the biggest thing that most Real Estate Agents don't understand and that's why most new agents fail. You have to spend money to make money. Remember you are a business and no one is going to get you business except you.

In this section we are going to discuss how to get business. What works and what doesn't, also where to spend your money and how to spend your time and not waste it. There are several avenues you can take and it's up to you to decide the things you want to do to get business. I am going to give you my opinion of how each thing works. I have been in the business for 20 years and have tried most everything. Also I have wasted a lot of time doing things that don't work, a lot of which my broker taught me.

DIRECT MAIL

This is where I put all my money to get business. There are several websites that you can go to make your own postcards. If you want to mail letters you can make them yourself. The website I use is Quantummail.com. They will even mail postcards for you or ship them to you to mail.

The reason I like direct mail is because I can control where my advertising goes and can target what area I want to sell in. One of the main things to consider when selling Real Estate is what you want to sell. What type and what price house do you like. That's what you need to be selling.

I know that people usually get direct mail and throw it in the trash, but you have a better chance of them seeing it than in a newspaper ad. That's why it is important to have a good advertising message. We will discuss that later in the advertising section.

OPEN HOUSES

Holding an open house is a good way to meet people and hopefully get new leads. This is one of the biggest things a broker will have a new agent do. It can be very time consuming without many results. In the last 20 years I can count how many sales I got from open houses on my fingers. You have to talk to at least 10 people before you find someone actually interested in buying a house. I also have had many open houses where no one showed up. I hold an open house mainly to satisfy the seller of one of my listings. I also can hand out my business cards and ask if the person has a house to sell. It's up to you to decide if you want to put time into an open house. Remember you need 24 sales a year to gross $60,000 a year and that should be your goal. It's going to be hard to get that many sales from holding open houses. I personally would rather spend the time at home with my family. However it is a way to maybe get some business without spending any money.

FRIENDS AND RELATIVIES

You need to let everyone know that you are in the

Real Estate Business. You should post this information on all of your networking sites such as facebook, myspace , and twitter. People that know you will send business to you.

Remember that your goal is to sell at least 24 houses a year and you're probably not going to get near that many leads from your friends and relatives. Also let me caution you that a real estate transaction can be stressful and you could lose a friend in the process. I sell to people I don't know so I can keep it to a strictly business relationship.

FLOOR TIME AT THE OFFICE

As I mentioned before you're office might offer floor time. This is where you are on a schedule at the office where you get sales calls that comes into the office. This is only at an office that has an open floor. A closed floor is where all buyers calls go to the listing agent. You can still get listing calls on a closed floor. Some companies operate this way while most offices have an open floor. Your broker will probably tell you this is a good way for a new agent to start. I agree and disagree. You can end up wasting a lot of time and find yourself being the secretary and the only one at the office on the weekends. I quit doing floor time years ago because I felt that the business I got verses the time I put in was not worth it. I also only want to work in the area and price range that I want to work in. Some of the calls I would get would be on some listing about 40 miles away. I think it is very important that you only work in the area you want to work in.

WEBSITES

Getting business from having your Website is very difficult. I have seen new agents spend $1000 or more to set up their own website. The fact is that it is so hard to get traffic to the website because there are thousands out there. The company setting it up and getting paid for it will almost promise you that they will generate traffic to your website. This is almost always not true. You can spend that money for so many other things. Later when you are successful you can have your own website. It can be a good tool to show your seller.

NEWSPAPER AND MAGAZINE

Running newspaper and magazine ads to get business is not a very productive way to spend your money. It is very expensive and produces very little. Also when promoting yourself you have to very careful what you say and most always has to be approved by your broker. You have to think about how is your ad going to be different than everyone elses and how are you going to get people's attention. You have to be offering something that people want and your ad has to be at least a half page in size. Like I said this is very expensive. I have seen agents be successful in running these ads, but they are usually already successful agents and have the money.

EXPIRED LISTINGS AND FOR SALE BY OWNER

Many agents call expired listings and for sale by owner listings to try to get business. This again is one of the many things that a broker will tell a new agent to do. The problem is that every other agent in the area is doing the same thing. Usually a listing is expiring because it was listed to high in the first place so it probably wouldn't be a good listing for you even if you did get it. Also a for sale by owner is usually selling the property themselves because they don't want to pay a commission and more than likely owe too much on that property. This is why you don't see seasoned agents going after these listings.

COLD CALLING AND GOING DOOR TO DOOR

This is also something a broker might suggest to a new agent. This is very dangerous. First of all before you call anyone you should always have a no call list to check to see if the person is on it. You can get heavy fines for calling someone on the no call list. Going door to door is something agents use to do years ago. It is much too dangerous in today's world.

CHAPTER
3

WORKING

WITH

BUYERS AND SELLERS

1. WORKING WITH BUYERS
2. WORKING WITH SELLERS

WORKING WITH BUYERS

There are agents who like to work with buyers. There are agents who like to work with both buyers and sellers. Working with both is what most agents do. That is what your broker will suggest to all new agents.

I mostly only work with sellers and these are the reasons why. Buyers take up a lot of time and you have to spend a lot of time finding them. You can get buyer referrals from friends and relatives which is the best way, but mostly you have to find them yourself. Open houses and doing floor time at the office is the best way and this takes a lot of your time. It takes talking to 10 people who are interested in buying real estate to make one sale. I have seen these numbers work several times. I also worked for a national home builder and these were the numbers they worked with. They had to get 10 people to come to a model home before they got 1 sale. So you can see you would have to get 10 leads off of floor at the office or have 10 people come to an open house. You will find the Real Estate business is all about numbers. If you want 2 sales a month you would have to have 20 prospects and that's hard to do just holding open houses and doing floor at the office.

The other thing about working with buyers is that it takes a lot of time and gas to show them houses. A lot of times they want to see every house in their price range. It is so important that you make sure that they are qualified before you show them anything. Make them talk to a mortgage person and get a pre-qualification letter if they haven't got one already.

Again I have seen a lot of agents come into the business and fail. They spend money on getting their license, they buy a new car to haul buyers around, they buy an expensive web-site, an expense cell phone, expensive business cards, put their time in doing all of the same things every broker has a new agent do, sell 1 or 2 homes in 6 months time and leave the business broke and in debt.

This happens over and over because they don't have a plan and don't understand the numbers and expenses there are in being in the Real Estate business. They also don't understand that being a Real Estate Agent is a business and it takes time to build. Even if you were lucky enough to have a sale on the first day that you were in the business it would take a month or 2 before you get paid.

I once knew a Real Estate Agent that worked with only buyers. He worked about 50 hours a week, put 50,000 business miles on his car in one year and made less than $20,000. That's about $6000 he spent on gas alone not to mention the wear and tear on his car. That's why I don't work with many buyers. If I get a call on one of my listings from a potential buyer I will meet them at the property and if I can't sell them that property I ask if I can show them some other properties in the same area. If it is in the same area I will work with them. If not I will refer them to another agent. I will then call the other agent with the lead with the understanding they will pay me a 25% referral fee. That's what I do with most of my buyer leads. That is usually a $1000. to $1500 and I don't have to put in the time and expense. It's like having people working for me.

If you decide to work with buyers just be careful and not put too much time and money into each one. I have seen successful agents work with buyers. They usually work with both buyers and sellers and most of the time they are seasoned agents. It's up to you again how you decide how to run your business. I am trying to tell you the simple truth about the Real Estate business. I would like to see everyone be successful. That's why I am sharing with you what I have experienced in the past 20 years so you will not make the same mistakes that most people do. Again the Real Estate business is simpler than you think. It is all about the numbers and always has been.

WORKING WITH SELLERS

"List To Exist" is the motto of a lot of Real Estate Agents and Brokers and there is a big reason for that. If you don't have listings you won't have business. Even if you like working with buyers you are going to have to have listings to get them. A lot of buyer calls come from sign calls and advertising run in newspapers, magazines, and the company web-site that your broker will run for you on your listings.

Sellers take less of your time. Once you have listed their home for sale there is not a lot more to do until you get an offer for it. You do need to touch base with them and let them know how things are going such as how many agents have shown their home and the feedback you got from them.

This is my main source of business and the main source of any successful agents I have known. Your main goal should be getting listings. Learn how to advertise and market yourself to sellers to get listings. Again you are not going to get many listings setting around the office on floor duty. It's very seldom that a call comes into the office that a person wants to list their house. I have gotten listings from floor duty, but I had to be several hours to get one.

You have to go after listings. Drive through subdivisions in areas that you like. Places where you would like to buy a house or around where you live. It's always easier to sell something you like. It's best however to pick an area that is no older than 10 years, because it will be easier to get the houses to pass inspection once you sell them. You then need to check on the turnover in the area. You can do this by going to your local Multiple Listing Service , (MLS), and checking the number of houses that have sold in the area for the last year. You want an area that has at least a 5% turnover. Let's say you have an area of 1000 homes and the turnover is 5%. That would mean that you can expect about 50 homes will sell in that area in the next year. These are the listings that you want to go after. You then need to have a plan on how you are going to go after those listings.

You will need to put together a listing presentation. I am going to show you later how to do that. Once you put it together you can use it over and over and make changes to it as you go along. It will turn out to be your most important tool. You will need to practice it over and over.

You will need to offer your potential sellers more than your competition does to get the listing. People are not interested in what you have done or how many houses you have sold or what college you have graduated from. They are interested in what you can do for them. I have set through listing presentations of other agents where all they do is try to talk about themselves and what they have accomplished. The seller is not interested in this. They want to know what you are going to do to sell their house.

There are lots of things you can offer them. I was talking before about what your broker needs to let you do to run your business and this is what I am talking about. I will give you just a couple of examples. You can offer your sellers a guarantee. Tell them you guarantee if they are not satisfied with your service that they can cancel the listing agreement at any time. I know some agents that use this and they hardly ever have a cancellation. It makes the seller comfortable with you and other agents in your area are not doing this. You could also offer to sell their house at a lower commission. This is something that you need to do when you first start to help you get listings. I have taken listings at 4 1/2%. I take 2% for the listing side and offer the buyers side 2 ½% which is usually posted in the MLS for other agents. You need to do this to get other agents to show the property. This is a big selling tool! You can tell your seller that a lot of agents are charging 7% and this could save them thousands. You could also charge 5% which is also a good savings. Listings are so important even though you took the listing at a lower commission just think what you could get out of it. You will get all the buyers calls, depending on the broker, and your name on the sign in the front yard and all the calls from the advertising on the web.

CHAPTER

4

ADVERTISING

1. SPEND MONEY TO MAKE MONEY

2. FARMING

SPEND MONEY TO MAKE MONEY

"You Have to Spend Money To Make Money" Advertising will be your biggest expense. I worked for a broker for many years who also sold Real Estate himself. He consistently made $100,000 a year from his personal sales and spent $20,000 a year advertising to get the business. He spent most of it on direct mail and some in magazines.

When you advertise you must have a message to your advertising that will get people to call you. You also have to select where you are going to advertise. If you work for a broker you have to have all advertising approved by him or her. This is advertising mainly in newspapers and magazines. For example your broker wouldn't want you to run an ad in the paper that you were offering a discount on your commission because other Real Estate Companies would see it and it might start a price war. That's why I put all my money in direct mail. It is sent to individuals that own homes and not advertised to the public. Newspaper and magazine advertising is good for advertising your listings but not good for getting business.

When you advertise you must give people a reason to call you. I have often seen ads in the newspaper where a agent puts in a picture of herself holding a dog and offering you a free CMA . First of all it was just an accident I saw it because it was so small and on page 12. Second of all, most people don't even know what a CMA is. This is an example of wasting money on advertising.

When I advertise with my direct mail post cards or one of my letters I make offers such as,
Save Thousands!
Before You List Your Home For Sale Call Me
I Could Save You Thousands
Call Me Today
                     or
Special!
I Need Houses To Sell
That's Why I Am Offering A
Hugh Discount This Month
Call Me Today

These are just a couple of ways to get people to call you. These are also ads that you couldn't run in the paper, but you can send them to the homes you want to list.

Always check with your broker before running any ads. There should not be a problem. Once again this is your business and these are probably good things to discuss with the broker before you go to work for him. I don't suggest that you always reduce your commission on the listings you take because I don't, but I also still market my direct mail that way. I have known agents that would never lower their commission and think it is stupid to do so. They would rather set around the office and wait for someone to call or set on open houses and wait for people to show up. These are also the agents that have no business! Having a listing at a lower commission is better than having no listing at all.

When I do my direct mail advertising I don't share what I am doing with anyone. These are my ideas and other agents in the office don't need to know my secrets. I even put my home address on my direct mail postcards so any returns will be sent to my house. I do this for two reasons. 1. I can track my mailings and update my mailing lists, and 2. no one in the office will see what I am mailing out. You also should not share your ideas with other agents. You need to realize that they are your competition.

When you mail out direct mail always use a first class stamp. Don't use a bulk mail rate. Bulk rate mail usually is mixed with all the other junk mail on a given day and is harder to get noticed.

Some advertising companies will send your mail out for you. This is not a good idea. They use a bulk mailing rate plus you have no way to check for sure that it was mailed. You need to stamp and mail it yourself. That way you also know exactly when it was sent out.

FARMING

Farming in the Real Estate Business is all about finding prospects. You find an area where you would like to have houses to list for sale and you work that area. This area could be around where you live or where you would like to live. Try to pick an area that is no more than 10 years old because when you sell a house you have to get it inspected and the house will pass inspection a lot easier if it is less than 10 years old. Houses older than 10 years might have to have a roof replaced or an air conditioner replaced. This can be very expensive and cause a big problem in a Real Estate transaction.

Before you pick an area go to the MLS and find out how many houses sold in that area in the past year. The turnover needs to be at least 5%. That means if the area is 1000 houses there would be 50 houses sold in the past year. You will need at least this size area.

Once you have found an area you will need to send direct mail into that area regularly. There are two ways to do this. You can send direct mail to one area every month or you can have two areas and send direct mail to each every other month. It takes 7 mailings for a lot of people to recognize your name.

There are a lot of agents that have been very successful farming an area. I myself have been successful at this. People want to do business with people they know. When you send them mail on a regular schedule they begin to feel like they know you and that you know the area they live in. You become the expert of that area.

Farming an area in a good way to get business, but my experience tells me that you want to mail to random areas as well. The best way to do this is to send 1000 pieces of mail to your farm every other month. The other months send 1000 pieces of mail to other areas. Make it a different area each time. This is a way to spread your message. If you are offering something that the seller is interested in he or she will keep the mailing and call you later when they might decide to move. I have had people call me two years after they received my mailing. They might also tell a friend or relative that is ready to sell.

People in the Real Estate Business are always talking about contacting expired listings and For Sale By Owners. I have never seen any agent be real successful at this. By farming you automatically contact these people in the areas you mail to. You are even mailing to listings that other people have. If that listing expires before the house sells they might call you. It is legal for you to mail to houses that are already listed for sale by someone else. The rules are you have to mail to everyone in the area and you need to have a disclaimer on your advertisement stating that if your home is listed with another broker this is not a solicitation.

Farming can be a great way to build your Real Estate Business. It does not take a lot of time to put your mailing together. You need to make sure that you have a good marketing message on your direct mail. This message needs to offer the seller something that will make it worthwhile for them to call you. It also needs to be professional. I talked before about getting professional postcards from quantummail.com. You can put whatever kind of message you want on the postcard. Have them ship them to you for you to mail.

CHAPTER

5

LISTING

PRESENTATION

WHAT YOUR LISTING PRESENTATION

SHOULD LOOK LIKE

WHAT YOUR PRESENTATION SHOULD LOOK LIKE

The most important tool that you can have is a great listing presentation. This is what you are going to show a potential seller when you have an appointment with them. When you go on a listing appointment it is just like applying for a job. You are on a job interview with the seller. I have seen agents that simply just print up a CMA (Competitive Market Analysis) and show it to a seller on the listing appointment. That is the worst thing you can do. The seller wants to know what you are going to do to sell their house and how much it is going to cost them. You also have to convince them that you are better than other agents.

Your listing presentation should be about 7 to 10 pages including the CMA. It should be in color and be in a nice 3 ring binder. Once you have your presentation made you can use it over and over. The only thing you would have to change is the CMA. It is a good idea to leave your presentation with the seller after you have gone over it with them. It gives them great information about their home and shows them through the CMA what it is worth. Tell them you made it just for them and that they can keep it.

It is important that you do a good job on convincing them not to overprice their home. You should spend some time on your CMA and make sure that is very accurate.

Now I am going to go through each page and tell you what information you should have on each one.

Page 1

The only thing that is going to be on page 1 is the customers name and your name. There are 3 ring binders that have a plastic insert on the outside of the binder. That's where this information should be.

A CUSTOMIZED MARKETING PLAN FOR
YOUR COSTUMERS NAME
YOUR COSTUMERS ADDRESS
BY
YOUR COMPANYS NAME
YOUR NAME
YOUR PHONE NUMBER

This should be in large enough font to cover the biggest portion of the first page and it should be in color.

Page 2 and 3

These next 2 or 3 pages should be all about the company you work for. All companies have marketing material showing the benefits of why you should list your home with them. All you have to do is get copies of this material and plug it in to these 2 or 3 pages. You can use more pages on this if you want. Just be careful not to use too much information because it could be boring to the seller.

Page 4

This is a very important page. This is where you talk a little bit about yourself. Tell them where you come from, what education you have, and what some of your accomplishments are. You will then list the reasons why they should list their home with you. I will give you some examples of things I use.

REASONS TO LIST YOUR HOME
FOR SALE WITH ME

1.I OFFER A GUARANTEE

I guarantee you can cancel my listing at any time if you are not satisfied with my service.

You might think this is a risky offer, but it really isn't. I have seen very few listings canceled because of this offer and the sellers like it. You can tell them that you don't know of any other agent that offers this and you have seen sellers get trapped with a bad agent for 6 months because they had a listing agreement that they couldn't get out of.

2. I OFFER DISCOUNTS

I will sell your home for 4 ½ % of the selling price which could save you thousands and still give you full service. I know a lot of Real Estate Agents that are charging as much as 7%

I don't know what the going rate is in your state. In my state the going rate is 6% and sometimes 7%. I will usually go to 4 ½% offering the selling agent in the MLS 2 ½%. I will go to 5% sometimes and if I have a lot of listings I sometimes take this out. If you don't have an ample supply of listings you need to make this offer. You have to have listings to make it as a Real Estate Agent.

3. I OFFER PROFESSIONAL PHOTOGRAPHY OF YOUR HOME

I will have a professional photograph your home for all the advertising and the internet.

I have a photographer photograph my listings. I can usually get this done for about $150. It is the best money you will ever spend. The difference between pictures you take and what they take is a big difference. This really helps you sell the home. You have to realize that these pictures are going to be all over the internet and have to look better than other listings. At this point of the presentation you should have a 3 ring binder of photos of other homes done by your photographer to show you seller. The photographer you decide to use will provide you with these photos. You can tell the seller that most agents take the pictures themselves. They don't spend money on a photographer. You can also tell them how important it is to have professional pictures of their home on the internet and other advertising.

4.MARKETING

I advertise in over 20 Web-Sites and publications such as Homes and Land Magazine, The Real Estate Book, and The Local Newspaper.

These are just a few examples of what you can offer a seller to get the listing. You can come up with reasons yourself to put on this page. It's all about selling yourself and offering the seller things that will make them want to list their home with you.

Page 5

I ADVERTISE IN THESE WEB SITES AND PUBLICATIONS

This page should be a list of all the web-sites and publications that you advertise their home on. I know your company has a list of these and you should list individually each one of them on this page. They should take up the whole page. I know for sure that when you put the listing on the MLS that it automatically is sent to at least 20 web-sites and you should list everyone on the on this page. This impresses the seller and makes it look like you are spending a lot of money advertising his home and that you have a marketing plan.

Page 6 to the end of presentation

The last thing to do is the CMA. Use the last few pages for your CMA showing the seller what is for sale and what has been sold recently in their neighborhood. You can also put in a page from Zillow.com. This is a web-site that will evaluate homes and show a price. It is mostly very accurate. That way you can compare it with you CMA price. You can also tell the seller that this price is what the buyer sees. Most buyers will go to this web-site or one like it before they buy a house. It will help you convince the seller not to price their home too high. You should not take a listing more than 7% over the CMA price, however it is up to you. If you think you can get them to lower to price later go ahead and take it. It's good to have listings, but remember that you are going to put money into it and it has to be profitable for you.

As you can see your listing presentation is a very important part of your business and will make a difference whether you get a listing or not. I will tell you however that the biggest % of Real Estate Agents that I know do not have a good listing presentation. They just go in the home and wing it. So really you have less competition than you think.

It should not make you nervous to give a listing presentation. It might a first, but you will get better and better at it. You can practice it at home on your relatives or friends. Just think how simple it can be. You have your presentation all ready to go. All you have to do is set down with the sellers and read it to the seller.

CHAPTER

6

WAYS TO START YOUR REAL ESTATE BUSINESS

1.TWO WAYS TO START YOUR BUSINESS
2. START YOUR OWN REAL ESTATE COMPANY

TWO WAYS TO START YOUR BUSINESS

The first way is start full time with a Real Estate Company. Before you do this there are things to consider. You need to figure your finances. The first 3 to 6 months you might not have any income. Even if you were lucky enough to have a sale on your first day which is very uncommon it would take a month or 2 to get it closed and receive your commission. Therefore you need to figure how much money you would need to pay your bills for about 3 to 6 months. It's better to figure 6 months. You will also have the expense of your Real Estate License, joining the local board, paying your board dues, getting your business cards, etc. Your broker will have a list of these things and have each one costs.

One of the most important things to have money for is your advertising. I always figure a minimum of at least $500. a month to advertise to get listings. I have seen a lot of people fail simply because they did not have enough money to stay in the business. It's important to have enough money to pay your bills, but almost more important to have enough money to advertise.

Once you have decided you have enough funds to

get into the Real Estate business you should do everything you can to get both buyers and sellers. That means doing floor time at the office, doing open houses, and prospecting for every lead that you can get. Remember you are just starting out in the business and don't yet have the repeat business and referrals that seasoned agents have. That's why you need advertising to get the business. It takes a while to build your business. The second way is to start part time.

The second way to get into the Real Estate Business is to start part time. You can work on getting your Real Estate License while you continue on your present job. A lot of Real Estate Companies say they don't want part time agents but there are a lot of companies that will. This gives you the opportunity to get some experience without quitting your present job. It relieves some of the financial burden that is placed on new agents.

The best way to work as a part time agent is to go after listings. Spend some money on advertising to get listing appointments. These appointments can be scheduled on the week-ends or evenings. Once you get the listing and put it in the MLS there is not much to do until you get an offer from another agent. Once again you can present that offer to the seller in the evenings. This will help you get your business started without the financial burden of trying to keep your bills paid until you get a closing.

When you are starting in the Real Estate Business there is a lot of time where you will be doing nothing until you have some business. Your broker will make suggestions of things such as calling expired listings or for sale by owners and doing floor time at the office waiting for the phone to ring, but all of these things are non productive and don't pay you any money. That's why I don't like working with buyers because they take up to much time. I think it is really important you only work with sellers when you start in the business. They don't take up much of your time and you can be doing something else to make money while you are waiting for your listings to sell. I have known a lot of new agents who have had a part time job while building their Real Estate Business. You could start your Real Estate Business while working your full time job if you have one then switch to a part time job while you build your business. A lot of full time agents do other things to make money. A lot of them have part time jobs that they can do at home or on their own schedule. All you need is to be able to always answer your cell phone. Your phone is your business. Never tell a client you are a part time agent. You are a full time agent with a part time job. A Real Estate Agent works 24/7.

The main reason new Real Estate Agents fail is because of money. They can't stay in the business long enough to be successful. The Real Estate Business is your own business. You can start and continue to build your own clients. Nobody can take that away from you. Your clients will get you more business if you keep in touch with them. They will also call you 2 or 3 years from now when they want to buy another home. That's why it is so important to stay in the business.

HOW TO START YOUR OWN REAL ESTATE COMPANY

Your goal could certainly be to start your own Real Estate Company. While it is true that signing up with national companies like Century 21, Re Max, or Caldwell Banker can be an advantage when you are trying to get listings there are a lot of things you can offer by being an independent.

An example of this is the commission you charge. By not having to split your commission with a broker you can make a lot more money so you can list a house for sale, charge a lot less and still make more than you would if you were working for a broker. When you own your own Real Estate Business you are the broker. You can also advertise anything you want because you don't have to have a brokers permission. You can advertise in the newspaper that you are only charging 4 ½% commission to sell houses if you want to. These are some examples of what you can do if you own your own company.

Even though people probably haven't heard of your company you can tell them that you are offering them the same things that the big companies are offering. Since advertising is a big concern of a seller you can explain to them that they will get the same advertising exposure with you. The internet is the best place to advertise houses for sale. That is where most all buyers look for homes. When you place a home for sale on the MLS it automatically goes to several web-sites including a lot of the major companies. A lot of major companies advertise to go to their web-site to see all the listings. This includes all the listings you put on the MLS. You are basically giving the seller the same advertising exposure as anyone else and charging them a lot less. People always want to save money. That is what built Walmart and several other large companies. They gave people the same for a lot less. That is the advantage you have by owning your own company. You can save people money and still make more than you would working for a broker.

You can charge the same commission rate as other brokers, but it would be difficult to compete. You have to be offering more than the competition. People can be greedy, but you can work this to your advantage. I would suggest not charging more than 4 ½% commission. This would still make you $4500. on a $200,000 sale even if someone else sold it. It would also save the seller $5000. That is if they had listed it with another broker at 7%. This is a great selling point to the seller in your listing presentation. You could also put this commission rate on your direct mail advertising. SAVE THOUSANDS IF YOU LIST YOUR HOME FOR SALE WITH ME. This will get people to call!

One of the down sides to owning your own Real Estate Business is that you would have to pay for your own advertising on listings since most companies you work for pay to advertise your listings in newspapers and magazines. The good news is everything else you would need is not that expensive.

The first thing you would need to do is get your brokers license. I would suggest attending a Real Estate school for this. In my state you have to be a licensed Real Estate Agent for 2 years before you can get your brokers license. The next thing is to name your company and register it. You then need an office. You can rent a space from a title company or a lawyers office fairly cheap. All the other things can be at home in your home office. You will need a computer, copier, and fax machine. Your cell phone will be your office phone. The only time you go to the office you rent is to meet with clients.

When you own your own Real Estate Company you can also hire other agents to work for you and receive a commission split when they sell a home. You can grow your company as big as you want.

That is really all you need to start your own Real Estate Company. It is not really expensive compared to other businesses where you have to get a large business loan to buy equipment and inventory. You can start fairly cheaply and you have a life time to build your business.

CHAPTER

7

KNOW YOUR NUMBERS AND YOUR COMPETITION

1.BY THE NUMBERS

2.KNOW YOUR COMPETITION

BY THE NUMBERS

The Real Estate business is all about numbers. I have said this before, but I can't say it enough. It's only when you understand the numbers that you can figure out what you need to do to get the amount of business that you want to get each year. It would be nice if you could just tell your friends and relatives that you are in the Real Estate business and they would send you business. That is certainly something you need to do but you have no idea how much business that would be. If you have a goal of selling 24 houses a year you probably are not going to get that much business from your friends and relatives.

When I worked for a builder they knew they would have to get 10 people to come to a model home before they got 1 sale. I can personally tell you that that was true. Therefore they had to do a certain amount of advertising to get the number of people to come to visit a model home to get the sales they wanted.

It is the very same formula for working with buyers. If you work with buyers and want 12 sales a year you will have to talk to 120 people a year that are interested in buying a home. You then have to plan on how you are going to do that.

It is a little different working with sellers. You have to do a fair amount of advertising. You have to spend approximately $20. in advertising for each $100.that you make. To have enough listings to sell 12 homes a year you would have to send out 1000 direct mail advertisements per month. The cost of this would be about $500.a month. This would be $6000.spent on advertising a year and you would make about $30,000 gross. Your cost would be 20%. These numbers could be more or less depending on the price of the houses and the commission you received for each one.

As you can see you have to know the numbers before you can make a plan to make the money you want to make. My former broker had his plan down perfect. He knew exactly what he had to do each year to make $100,000. He did it consistently year after year and knew exactly how many listings he had to have to make that income. He also spent $20,000.a year in advertising.

You also have to have a plan. Not only do you have to have a plan to get business, but you have to have a plan to stay in the business. You need to figure out how much money you have to live on until you get your first sales commission and how much money you have for advertising. Remember once again that being a Real Estate Agent is not just a sales job, it is a business.

KNOW YOUR COMPETITION

When you are in the Real Estate Business you have to know what your competition is. Just like any other business you have to be competitive to get business. There are lots of other companies trying to get the same houses to list in your area. That is why I have said that you have to offer something that other agents are not offering to get the business. Most agents don't understand this. They go after business offering the same thing as everyone else in the area is offering.

There are lots of things that have changed in the Real Estate Business. You can't do all the things that you used to do in the old days to get business. A lot of brokers are stuck in the past and continue to do the same things they did years ago. They don't even understand what their competition is.

You would think that the big Real Estate Companies would be your main competition however with the use of computers and the internet it makes it a lot easier for people to set up their own Real Estate Business. When they set up their own company they can set their own commission rates and offer the seller anything they want to get the listing. They can be a strong competition.

There are other companies like Assist To Sell and For Sale By Owner that offer a lot of the same things. A lot of companies advertise they will list your home in the MLS for $495.00. When they get the appointment they explain to the seller that is only the listing side in the MLS. You also have to offer the buyers agent a commission around 3%. By listing the house in the MLS for $495.00 the seller has no service from the listing agent. The seller has to show the property, advertise the property, and do the Real Estate contract. The seller can save a lot of money doing it this way but they usually end up listing the property with the agent at full service and full commission to the listing agent.

These are the kind of things that brokers in large companies won't allow you to do. Some day they are going to wake up and realize that they need to offer their customers more choices and programs to get their business. Listing a property for $495.00 is not very profitable, however you still get the MLS sales calls and you might sell the house and receive a 3% buyers commission. Plus you will get the full listing price if the owner decides to list it with you at full service and full commission. Your competition is doing this and being very successful.

I don't expect you will be able to do these kinds of things if you go to work for a large company and that's OK. It is very important that they allow you to lower your commission to get listings when you are starting out. Just explain to them that you won't advertise in the newspaper or magazines that you offer a lower commission, but you would like to offer a discount in your direct mail advertising.

CHAPTER

8

BUILDING REFERRALS

1. BUILDING A REFERRAL LIST

2. DON'T TAKE THINGS PERSONAL

BUILDING A REFERRAL LIST

To be successful in the Real Estate Business you need to know lots of people. Most of them you will like and build a relationship with. There will also be some that won't like you for various reasons. That is just the way it is when you work with people. You can't please everyone.

To get referrals you need to make a list of everyone you know. You can do this on a excel spread sheet. List everyone you can think of including friends, relatives, and people you do business with. List their name, address, phone number, and e-mail address. Keep adding to the list every time you meet someone. An example of this is when you are setting on a open house you can get the names and addresses of everyone that you meet and add them to your list.

These will be the people you know list. You should send them a postcard about 4 times a year. This could be around holidays or just to say hi and let them know you are in the Real Estate Business. You will be surprised how fast your list will grow. Every time you make a sale you can add their name to the list. You also should call them from time to time to see if they know anyone that is interested in buying or selling Real Estate.

It's takes time to build a Real Estate Business. The longer you are in it, the more people you will know and the more referrals you will get. This will be your business and nobody can take that away from you.

The second list you should make is the people you don't know. This could be your farm area. This should be a list of 1000 to 2000 people and you need to send mail to them every month. After you send mail to them a least 6 times they will begin to recognize your name.

I send half of my direct mail to my farm area and half to random areas each month. This gets my name out there and spreads my message. I keep track of each mailing. I get my mailing list from the MLS. There is a way in the MLS I use to get a mailing list of names from the tax records. Once I build that list I can save it to my computer. That way I can track and date my mailings even to my farm area.

You need to know people to be successful in this business. This is the way to build your business. There are several organizations you can join to meet people. Find your local Chamber of Commerce web-site and look for a schedule of networking meetings. These are meetings that are usually held at a local restaurant on a regular basis. There are all kinds of professional people there. They are all looking for the same thing. They are there to meet people that will help their business.

If you have children, be active in school events. I have known several successful soccer moms. If you are retired, go to your local senior citizens organization. Go to all the garage sales in your neighborhood. These are just a few ways to meet people. If you think about it you can come up with a lot or ideas on your own.

Don't Take Things Personal

As you work with many different people such friends, relatives, and referrals you need to never take things personal and always keep things on a business level. This is sometimes very hard to do because you are dealing with lots of emotions and situations when it comes to selling a persons home. In all the years I have only had one bad customer. I had met this couple at an open house. They decided that they wanted to move and called me later to list their house for sale. It took 2 months to get a contract on their home. They then were ready to look for another home to buy. The husband went overseas to work a job with his company. I started showing the wife houses that they might be interested in buying. One day she called and said she was going to start working with another agent. There was no reason that I could think of that she would do this. I had been showing her houses and everything was fine. I had a good relationship with her husband. She even had her husband call my office and tell my broker I wouldn't show her the houses she wanted to see. I was very upset and could not figure out what happened. I even had my broker take over the deal and I did not even go to the closing of their home. I found out later that she ran into a friend she had not seen for a long time. This friend just happened to have just got a Real Estate License and talked her into buying a house from her. This did not have anything to do with me not showing her houses. She lied to her husband to make me look bad so she could work with her friend. That just shows you why you should not take things personal.

There are a lot of people that have a Real Estate License. A lot of them have not sold a home in a long time until they run into a friend that wants to buy or sell a home. That is why they keep their license active.

I have been on a lot of listing appointments that I thought went real well. The sellers seem to like me and what I was offering. If they did not list the house with me on that appointment I would tell them I would call them in a few days for their decision. Sometimes they would tell me they had decided to go with something else. This did not make since to me since everything had gone so well on my appointment with them.

You will find out that it is not anything that you have personally done to not get a listing. A lot of people end up listing with a friend of theirs and just wanted you to come out so they would have a comparison. I have had people list their house For Sale By Owner after they met with me. It is usually true that it wasn't anything you did personally, however you will run into some people that just won't like you for some reason and there is nothing you can do about it. People might want to do business with someone older or younger than you or maybe your personality clashes with theirs. This is why you need numbers to work in your favor. You will not get every listing and you need all of the listing appointments you can get.

Real Estate transactions can get very emotional. I do believe in referrals from friends and relatives. I have also sold homes to friends and relatives. It is hard to turn down a sale. I will caution you that it can also be very difficult at times. You might even lose a friend or cause a lot of trouble in your family. If anything goes wrong even if it is not your fault, you will get the blame. Don't take it personal!

CHAPTER
9

PROFESSIONAL RELATIONSHIPS AND TECHNOLOGY

1. PROFESSIONALS TO HAVE ON YOUR SIDE
2. TECHNOLOGY

PROFESSIONALS TO HAVE ON YOUR SIDE

There are certain professional people you need to help you with your business such as title closers, lawyers, home inspectors, mortgage representatives, bankers, photographers, and home repair businesses. You should interview each one to make sure that they are the person you want to do business with. It is good business practice to have a good relationship with them because they could also send you business.

When you are selling Real Estate you need to use either a title company or a lawyer to close your Real Estate transactions. Some states require a lawyer to close a Real Estate transaction while others will allow you to use a title company. This person is very important to you. Once you write a Real Estate contract you turn it over to the closing person. If it is your listing the seller usually gets to pick the closing company. They usually will close with who you suggest. It's fine to use a title company; however it can be an advantage closing with a lawyer. They both charge around the same price. When using a lawyer you can sometimes get free legal advice if anything should go wrong with the contract or the lawyer can write the addendums that you might need. Whatever you decide try to stay with the same person. They will do a better job for you if they know you are going to give them future business.

You need a good home inspector. This person is picked by the buyer to inspect the home before they close. You need to pick one that does a good job but does not go overboard. I have seen a lot of home inspectors cause the deal to fall apart because they did too good of a job. They found little things wrong with the home that really were not important. Before you decide what inspector to use ask some seasoned agents around the office who they use.

Mortgage representatives and bankers can be a big help to your business. They might even help you with some advertising money on a listing or print up flyers about financing to display inside the listing. They also have sign riders that they can put on your listing sign in front of the home. Sometimes a buyer will call them first to see if they qualify to buy the home. Again you need to establish a relationship with them and let them know that you are going to send all your business to them. They will try hard to get all of your Real Estate transactions financed.

A home repairman is a good person to get to know. You might have things to fix on a home after inspection. Make sure the person is licensed and insured. Again ask around the office for a list of repairmen that other agents have used.

A professional photographer can be of great help getting the home sold. They have the equipment to make the pictures of the home look like they just came out of a magazine. In about 90% of homes that are sold, the buyer first saw the home on the internet. It is important that the pictures look better than the competition.

TECHNOLOGY

There is new technology coming out all the time. A lot of this is helpful to a Real Estate Agent. We need computers, cell phones, and fax machines just to name a few. I remember when the new listings posted in the MLS would come out every two weeks in the form of a book. Now we can post them instantly on the MLS through the computer.

You can also have too much technology. When you are a new agent you will be flooded with people wanting to sell you a new form of technology to help your business. A lot of these are unnecessary and causes you to spend money that you could be using for advertising.

I have seen new agents spend thousands on websites, I phones, e-mail campaigns, and fancy business cards, none of which is going to help them get business. You need to keep it simple and only spend money on the basics especially when you are starting out in the business. You have enough expenses just paying for your license fees and MLS dues.

The biggest thing in technology that is very helpful and is not expensive is social networking sites. Sites such as facebook and myspace just to name a few are a great ways to let people know that you are in the Real Estate Business.

CHAPTER
10

REAL ESTATE BOOKS,

REAL ESTATE SCHOOLS

AND

SEMINARS

1.REAL ESTATE BOOKS
2. REAL ESTATE SCHOOLS
3. SEMINARS

REAL ESTATE BOOKS

It is important to learn as much about the Real Estate business as you can. One way is to read Real Estate books. There are a lot of Real Estate books out there and there are a lot of bad ones. I have only read one in the past 20 years that I learned anything about the business. Most of them go on and on for 300 pages about the same things over and over. They all say call For Sale by Owners, call expired listings, call your friends, and knock on doors. None of these will help you make it in the Real Estate business.

I continue to read books hoping to find out new ways to make my business better. The last one I read was the worst one yet. This Real Estate agent said that she made a lot of money calling expired listings. She said she got in the office at 6:30 am in the morning and got the expired listings from the MLS. She said there would be about 100 of them and she would spend the next hour or so looking up all the phone numbers so she could call them.

First of all I have never in 20 years seen an agent come to the office at 630 an in the morning. Second of all she must have a huge MLS because 100 expired listings a day is a lot. Third, even if she did have that many, a huge amount of them would be listings that nobody would want. There is a reason that listing don't sell in the first place. Fourth, she would need to screen all the numbers against the no call list. There are big fines for calling people on the no call list. Finally, if she gets all the phone numbers that she can call, which will not even be close to 100 because of the no call list, is she actually going to call these people starting at 9 or 10 am in the morning?

These are the kind of books that get new agents in trouble. They spend time and money getting their license and end up doing all the wrong things to get business. There are very few things out there to teach you the Real Estate business. You would think your broker would train you to be successful but this is very rarely true. Most of them teach all the same old things like the example I gave you about the book.

REAL ESTATE SCHOOLS

It is best to select a Real Estate School to attend to train you how to get your license. There are on-line courses you can take, but I have seen people be a lot more successful when they actually attend a school. The school will also offer continuing education classes that you might need every 2 years.

Your local Board of Realtors a lot of times offer courses on different Real Estate subjects. These are great ways of learning how to improve your business.

SEMINARS

As a Real Estate agent you will be getting a lot of invitations to attend Seminars. These are usually posted in the office and a lot of times they are free. Don't waste your time or money on these. They are only going to try to sell you something that costs a lot and won't help you with your business. The only Seminar I went to they were trying to sell Television advertising and an 800 phone number with an automatic message. The cost was $4000. They kept saying only 1 sale will pay for it. As I said, don't waste your time.

CHAPTER

11

EXAMPLES OF SUCCESSFUL
REAL ESTATE AGENTS

1. AGENT 1
2. AGENT 2 AND 3
3. AGENT 4 AND 5

AGENT 1

Here are just a few short stories of successful Real Estate agents that I have known.

Agent 1 has been in the business for about 15 years. He owns a national company franchise. He is not successful because he owns his own company. He gives all the sales calls and leads that come into the company to his agents. He generates his own leads for the sales he does. He consistently makes $100,000 plus per year in good times and bad just off of his personal sales. He is a listing agent and works with very few buyers. He usually refers his buyer calls to an agent for a referral fee. He spends over $20.000 a year on advertising for his personal sales. He buys a full page ad in the Homes and Land magazine every month which costs about $800. Homes and Land is a national magazine which advertises local listings and has national advertising on the web. He spends the rest of his advertising money on direct mail. He sends about 400 pieces of direct mail to the area around every home he sells. He knows exactly how much advertising he has to do to consistently get the same number of sales each year. He has a wonderful listing presentation. He has a professional photographer take the pictures of all his listings. He has a lawyer do all of his closings.

He has 50 to 70 listings at one time. He is very successful

AGENT 2

Agent 2 has been in the Real Estate Business for about 10 years. She almost totally relies on direct mail to get her new business. She does run a ¼ page ad in the Homes and Land Magazine, but that is mostly to just advertise her listings. She only has her listing appointments in the afternoon. Her mornings are set aside to do her advertising for new listings. Every morning she mails out 200 postcards. She mails to her farm area as well as new areas. She does not offer any commission reduction. Her postcards are about her just listed properties and her success as a Real Estate Agent. She grosses around $80,000 to $110,000 a year. She has her office at home and very rarely goes to the main office. She has offers on her properties faxed to her home. Once she has finalized the offers she sends them to her assistant. The assistant then does all the things necessary to get the contract closed. She very rarely works with buyers unless it is on one of her properties.

AGENT 3

Agent 3 is what I call the lucky agent. Her kind of success is very rare but it could happen to anyone. When she was just starting out as a Real Estate Agent she was setting on an open house one Sunday. A gentleman walked in and said he was moving to the area. He loved the home she was holding open and ended up buying it. Come to find out he was the new relocation director of the biggest corporation in the city. He gave her all the relocation business of the corporation from that time on. This also included not only people coming into the city but people moving out. That was 10 years ago and she still is getting the business. I don't know what her income is but I would guess around $200,000 a year. She buys 3 pages of advertising every month in the Homes and Land Magazine at a cost of $2400. She has about 70 listings at one time and she does work with buyers as well as sellers.

AGENT 4

Agent 4 got her Real Estate license and went to work for a builder just before the Real Estate boom.

She sold new homes in a subdivision of about 800 homes. When the market slowed down she went to work for a national Real Estate company. By selling new homes she had already built a pretty good sized referral list. She began to work on getting resales in the same subdivision that she had sold new homes in. She was very successful. She now runs a full page ad every month in the Homes and Land Magazine at a cost of $800. , a full page ad in the local newspaper that is mailed to 10,000 homes each month in and around the subdivision she farms at a cost of $1000. a month, and direct mail. Her income is over $100,000. a year. She has built a good business.

AGENT 5

Agent 5 owns her own Real Estate business. She started out working for a national company. She then got her brokers license and started her own company. Since she owns the company she is free to advertise anything she wants to without another brokers permission like you would have to do if you worked for another broker. Her whole marketing plan is built around charging a lower commission to sell homes. She advertises that she can save the seller thousands by listing their home with her. She even puts this in her ad that she runs in the newspaper. She has an advantage over a national company because they would never advertise a lower commission rate in the paper because they are afraid other national companies would do the same. She has no competition in this area and she offers the seller the same service. She runs a 1/2 page ad every month in the Homes and Land magazine at a cost of $600., a 1/2 page ad in the local paper mailed to 10,000 people in her farm area at a cost of $600., and she spends about $1000. a month on direct mail. She makes over $100,000. a year.

The above successful agents all have a plan and all spend money to make money. They all know how much and what kind of advertising they need to do to get the results they need. They don't wait for someone else to get them business, they get it themselves.

AN UNSUCCESSFUL AGENT

Along with all the successful agents I also know lots of unsuccessful agents. I will give you an example of one. This agent goes to the office every day about 8:00 and stays until 4:00. He takes everyones floor time that doesn't show up. He does not spend a dime on advertising. He would never lower his commission. He does set on open houses on Sundays. He puts in at least 50 hours a week and has an annual salary of about $20,000. I have seen several agents do the same things and they are usually gone from the business in less than 6 months. A lot of agents go to different companies because they think it's the companies fault they weren't successful. These people are the majority of the Real Estate agents working today. The only one good thing about this is this is your competition. Even though there are a lot of Real Estate Agents out there it's not that hard to compete with them.

CHAPTER

12

THE MLS

AND

COMMISSION RATES

1. THE MLS
2. COMMISSION RATES

THE MLS

The Real Estate Multiple Listing Service (MLS) is where Real Estate agents list their properties for sale. It is the most valuable tool that a Real Estate agent has for selling a house. When you list a property for sale in the MLS you are advertising the property to every Real Estate agent in a given area. The MLS can carry 5000 to 15000 and even more properties for sale.

This is a lot of free advertising. You are not only advertising to the other Real Estate agents in the area you are advertising to the public as well. The MLS also has a public web site. Potential buyers can go to this site and view all the properties for sale. They can put in what price and area they want to look at. Your name and contact information comes up on the listing so they can call you if they are interested. The MLS listings also go to lots of other web-sites. The MLS does what they call a push every day. This means they send all the updated information every day to these web-sites. Realtor.com is just one of them. That means that the information is getting viewed by potential buyers nationwide.

It has been my experience that at least 90% of

homes are sold through the MLS.

COMMISSION RATES

The Real Estate business has changed and so have commission rates. In 1987, when I started, the commission rates where 7%. Nobody ever talked about anything lower. Lots of agents even thought that it was a state law or something. The truth is that it is legal to charge any fee you want when you are a broker.

When I came to Florida just about all of the companies were charging 6%. Then the Real Estate market got hot and properties were selling fast. It was hard to get listings because there was so much competition for them. That is when we saw the first 4% listing. Once it got started there were a lot of companies charging 4%. That is when for sale by owner companies got popular by charging a flat fee to help people sell their home. The biggest problem for them is that they could not list them in the MLS. Then the companies that would put the listings in the MLS for a flat fee came along. The seller would still have to offer the selling agent a commission. This was still cheaper for the seller. These companies had different programs they could offer the seller at different prices. There was one fee for if the seller would want to sell it themselves and another fee if they wanted the company to help them.

The Real Estate Company I worked for at the time would not let the agents charge the low fee of 4%. Since they were getting a cut of the commission the lower rate would bring less money to them. The broker has control over what rate the agent charges. That made it hard to get listings since so many other companies were charging 4%. I went to another company.

This is a prime example of not having control of your business because of your broker. You need to be able to make your own decisions about your own business. You are the one paying for all of your expenses. That is why the right broker is so important. You need to be able to set your own commission rates. I had no problem finding a broker with a national company that let me take listings at 4%. If I hadn't found a national company I would have found a smaller company. It is always better to have a national company to work for, but if you can't find one that will let you run your own business you are better off going to work for a smaller company.

There are a lot of smaller companies these days. They can offer the seller basically the same services. Because of the internet they can advertise just as much as the larger companies do. In fact the bigger companies advertise they show all the listings. This includes the listings of the smaller companies as well. That is a big selling tool when the smaller company is talking to a seller about getting a listing. Smaller companies are big competition because they can offer to do the same job cheaper.

A lot of agents argue that a lower commission hurts the sale of the home. They say the agents in the MLS will not show the home because it offers a lower rate. This is not true. The buyers usually find the homes they are interested in on the internet and then ask the agent they are working with to show them those homes.

CHAPTER

13

YOUR TIME IS VALUABLE

1.HOW TO MAKE THE BEST USE OF YOUR TIME

2.BE PROFESSIONAL

HOW TO MAKE THE BEST USE OF YOUR TIME

A big part of the Real Estate business is learning how to use your time. You can spend a lot of time doing nothing which will hurt the grow of your business. You can see this when you go into a Real Estate office. A lot of the agents are just hanging out there because they have nothing else to do. In fact there is very little to do at the Real Estate office to help you get business.

You need to learn how to use your time the right way to make the most money. The way to do that is go back to the numbers. This is another example of how important listings are. It takes less time to list houses than it does to sell them. When you work with a buyer it takes a lot of time. You first have to find a buyer, then you have to get them qualified, and then you have to find them a home. All the time you are going to put in is going to result in only one sale and that could take weeks. You can only work with 2 or 3 buyers at a time. You could take days just hauling 1 buyer around to show them houses. You will feel like you are working hard but you are not making any money and you are using up all your time.

When you list a home you will need to put in very

little time until you get an offer on it. You will also have time to list a lot more. It's not uncommon to see successful agents have as many as 50 listings or more at a time. You can manage that many at one time because they are not all going to sell at once. By having listings you also automatically have people working for you. Since the listings are in the MLS you will have other agents showing your properties. Let them put in the time and burn up their gas so you won't have to. Not only are you getting the most out your time, but you are getting other peoples time as well.

A lot of millionaires say the way to make money is to have other people working for you and that is what you are doing when you have listings.

   This is very important information when you are starting out. The easiest and cheapest way to start in the Real Estate business is listing houses. You can work a full or part time job until you get enough sales to go full time. Some people have the money to start in the Real Estate Business and have enough money to pay their bills for at least 6 months until they get a commission, but most people that I have seen don't. If you start part time and just list houses you will be able to stay in the business and that is what most people can't do.

That's why there is such a big turnover in the business. The best situation to be in is to be able to pay your bills and expenses by just working part time until you get your business built and that could be at least 2 years. That is why it is so important to get the most out of your time. Most full time agents I have seen have more than enough time each week to work a part time job because of their time wasted hanging out at the office.

BE PROFESSIONAL

Another way to make the best use of your time is to be professional in everything you do. A lot of people never think if this as a way to make the best use of your time, but it is very important. You are going to have to spend money on advertising to get listing appointments. It is important that you don't waste your time on that appointment. You need to show up at the appointment looking your best just like it was a job interview. That is what it really is, a job interview. People are going to hire you to sell their house.

Your listing presentation needs to look very professional as well. It needs to be very informative as well looking good. Your presentation always needs to be in color. You need to offer to have their home photographed by a professional photographer and you need to show them a sample of his or her work.

A persons home is a lot of times the most valuable thing that they own. That is why they want to list their home for sale with a professional that they can trust to do a good job in selling it. This is a big transaction.

As you can see being professional in what you do can help make sure you are making the best use of your time.

CHAPTER

14

WHERE THE REAL ESTATE MARKET IS HEADED

1.PAST MARKET

2.THE REAL ESTATE BOOM

3.THE PRESENT MARKET

PAST MARKET

When I started in the Real Estate business was in 1987. The market was fairly stable. Then the interest rate went to 16%. That made it very hard to sell houses. Later when the interest rates started to come down the market picked up again. The interest rate then was 8% to 10%. That seemed to work fine. The interest rate does not affect people buying houses as much as it affects the prices of homes. People will buy what they can afford and when the interest rate is high that just means that Real Estate prices have to come down for people to qualify.

This market continued through the 90s. Everything was going fine. People could qualify for home mortgages and home prices appreciated about 7% to 8% a year. This also made it a good investment for the owner.

It was a good time to be a Real Estate agent. People were selling and people were buying. It was fairly easy for a Real Estate agent to figure out how he or she was going to get the sales they needed to get each year to make the income they wanted to make. Even though Real Estate can be somewhat of a roller coaster ride, things seemed to be level all through the 90s.

THE REAL ESTATE BOOM

I had been in the Real Estate business for about 15 years when the Real Estate boom began. I started in Missouri and was now in Florida. I thought I had seen most every kind of Real Estate market there was. I was very surprised by what happened. I am still not sure how it happened. All of a sudden the market picked up. It seemed like everyone could get a mortgage by just signing their name. Houses started selling fast and that created a shortage of homes on the market. The shortage caused prices to go up. At that time the investors came into the picture and flipping became popular. They would buy a house and sometimes sell it before they closed on it for a higher price. This caused home prices to go up at a rate of 30%.

It was a hard time to be a Real Estate agent because even though homes were selling quick there was a flood of people getting their Real Estate license. It was hard to get listings because everyone was competing for them. That is when agents started offering to list houses for 4%.

I was very concerned about this market. For years Real Estate prices had always been based on the income of the buyers in a given area and what they could qualify for. There was no way the average income in the area I lived in could support these kinds of prices. Since the mortgage companies were writing these mortgages based on a lower payment to start with and a bigger payment later. They were also qualifying the buyers at the lower payment and sometimes the buyer would only have to state their income and would not have to prove it. The results of this were the Real Estate market fell and prices declined. Three years later we are still trying to get the market balanced again.

THE PRESENT MARKET

Todays market is starting to get back to the market that it used to be. There are very positive things happening. It is a very good time to get into the business. Even though there are a lot of foreclosures the market is balancing. The foreclosures need to happen. People that own homes that they owe more on the home than what it is worth are realizing that the only thing to do is to let it go into foreclosure or give it back to the bank. I agree with this. A lot of people bought a house in good faith and could qualify for the house when they bought it. It was because the banks were making loans to people who couldn't afford it that drove the market prices up. It is not uncommon to see homeowners $100,000 upside down on their homes. It would take years to make up that difference. It is a moral issue with a lot of people that have always paid their bills, but it just makes good business sense.

These are the things that are going on in the market that will balance the prices and buyers will be able to qualify to buy a home easier. We are getting close to having a very stable market. Real Estate will always rebound and people will always be buying houses.

A lot of Real Estate agents got out of the business during the past 3 years. There is less competition now and it is a great time to start a Real Estate career.

CHAPTER

15

CLOSING

1.CLOSING AGENT
2.WORKING WITH ANOTHER REAL
ESTATE AGENT
3.PROTECT YOUR SELLER

CLOSING AGENT

After you negotiate a Real Estate contract and finalize the price and terms it is time to work toward closing the deal. This can be done with a title company or a lawyer. In most states either one is fine. In other states you have to use a lawyer. Both charge about the same. There benefits to have your own lawyer close your Real Estate transactions. You might need some legal addendums to close the transaction and the lawyer can do those for you. In most states you can pick the closing agent if you represent the seller. Whether you represent the seller or the buyer you should contact the closing agent regularly until the transaction is closed. There can be problems come up with the closing and the closing agent might not notify you right away because they are handling several closings at the same time.

If you have the seller in the Real Estate transaction the first thing you need to do before you take it to the closing agent is to verify the financing. If the buyer is getting a mortgage you need to have a pre qualification letter from the mortgage company and also call the mortgage representative to verify it. If it is a cash transaction you need to verify the funds by calling the buyers bank.

WORKING WITH ANOTHER REAL ESTATE AGENT

Most of your Real Estate transactions are going to be done with another Real Estate agent. Since the house is listed on the MLS the biggest percentage of sales are split between 2 Real Estate agents. Both agents will be working with the same closing agent. Do not assume that the other agent is going to do their job. This is real important when you have the seller. In most Real Estate contracts the buyer has 20 days to get a mortgage commitment from the mortgage company. This is not the pre qualification letter the buyer had to come up with in the beginning. It is the commitment letter to show they are going ahead with the mortgage. This is after they have appraised the property and have agreed to make the mortgage. If you don't have this on time there could be problems with the closing. You have to stay on top of this even though there is another agent involved. I have run into a lot of other Real Estate agents in the past 20 years that simply don't know what they are doing. I have always had to work with the closing agent closely to get my Real Estate closings done on time.

PROTECT YOUR SELLER

When I was selling Real Estate in Missouri the Real Estate contract was written for the contract to close on one day and the possession to be given to the buyer about a week later. This made sure the seller would get the money at closing and then the buyer would move in later. In the state of Florida and many other states the possession is given to the buyer at closing. This can cause many problems. If anything goes wrong with the closing being done on time, and it sometimes does, the seller can be in a very difficult position. I have seen this happen a lot of times. The sellers have already moved their furniture out of the house and are ready to close on their new house but they can't until they close on their old one. You should always know what the sellers situation is. If they need to close on another house right after the old one you can write an addendum to the contract. Have the sellers lease back their old house for a couple of weeks after they close. That way they will get their money and have 2 weeks to close on their new one. The buyers usually don't mind waiting a couple of weeks to take possession.

There are several things that can go wrong with a closing. That is why you have to stay in communication with everyone involved. Try to close your Real Estate transactions with the same people. The more they get to know you the more they will stay in contact with you during the closing process.

A lot of successful agents pay a person to close their transactions. They usually pay them about $250. You can usually find an agent around the office that will do this for you or some companies have people working for them that will do this for a price. It can save you a lot of time. Once you negotiate a contract you turn it over to them and they will work with the closing company to get it closed.

SUMMARY

Real Estate is a business. If you are going to be successful as a Real Estate agent you are going to have to put some money into it just as you would any other business that you would start. Most people try to start with nothing. They call expired listings, for sale by owners, set on open houses, and put time in at the office answering phones. There are a few that make it this way, but very few. They are usually gone from the business in a few months. You can't count on your broker to make you successful because they won't. They do of course want you to come to work for them full time because they are going to get a cut of your commission on anything you sell; however they are not paying you a salary. You are self employed.

After seeing all kinds of agents in the past 20 years I will tell you how I would get into the Real Estate business without wasting your time and money.

First you need to figure out your finances. You will need at least 6 months of income to pay your bills and at least $500. to $1000. a month for advertising. You will need at least $1000. for your license and MLS dues. If you don't have this much money you are going to have to start part time and keep a full or part time job until you get started making money. Even if you have the money it probably is best to start part time because you don't know for sure if you are going to like the business. Make sure that you do have the money to advertise.

Next I would interview with at least 4 Real Estate companies. Make sure they will let you lower your commission rate on listings. You might have to do this to get some listings to start with. Make sure they will pay for advertising on your listings, and most important make sure they will let you start part time.

Next it is time to get your license. Attend a good Real Estate school to show you how to pass your Real Estate exam. It will cost you some money, but I have seen a lot of agents try to do it on their own and end up taking the exam a lot of times before they pass.

Next it is important that you only concentrate on just getting listings. You don't need to work with buyers because they take up to much time. Since you are working another job until you get started making money at Real Estate you don't have time to work with buyers. You don't need to put in floor time at the office or set on open houses. You are going to get listings only. By putting your listings in the MLS other agents will be showing them. Let them put their time and money into working with buyers because you don't have time to right now. The most important to have right now is an awesome listing presentation and the money to advertise. These are things you will need anyway when you are successful enough to go full time so why not start with one thing at a time.

Next you will need to start advertising. I gave some examples of how to advertise in the advertising section of this publication. Drive through areas on the weekends when people are home and outside to see what kind of people live there and what kind of homes there are in the area. Pick areas you would like to live in. The good thing about listing properties you can pick the area you want to work in. Once you have picked an area go to the MLS and see what kind of turnover there is in that area. You want at least a 5% turnover in a year. You should have a lot more than one area to mail to. You can rotate between them if you want to.

The next thing to do is to start mailing to these areas. It might take a while before you starting getting phone calls for appointments. This is an investment in the business you are starting.

You also need to let everyone you know that you are in the Real Estate business. Use all the networking sites to contact your friends and relatives and get the word out there.

If you approach the Real Estate business this way you will be building yourself a business without taking too much risk. You will only be spending the money for advertising and you will still have an income from your other full or part time job. I know a lot of agents that have other jobs even though they have been in the business for a long time. The Real Estate business can still be an up and down business. You have to do what is necessary to make it through the bad times and be in the business when things are good.